EASTER
PIANO SOLOS
30 TRIUMPHANT HYMNS AND CLASSICAL PIECES

ISBN 978-1-4950-9711-9

Hal•Leonard®
7777 W. BLUEMOUND RD. P.O. BOX 13819 MILWAUKEE, WI 53213

In Australia Contact:
Hal Leonard Australia Pty. Ltd.
4 Lentara Court
Cheltenham, Victoria, 3192 Australia
Email: ausadmin@halleonard.com.au

Visit Hal Leonard Online at
www.halleonard.com

AIR
from WATER MUSIC

By GEORGE FRIDERIC HANDEL
1685–1759

Andante con moto

ALLEGRO MAESTOSO
from WATER MUSIC

By GEORGE FRIDERIC HANDEL
1685–1759

ALLELUIA
from EXSULTATE, JUBILATE, K.165
excerpt

By WOLFGANG AMADEUS MOZART
1756–1791

Allegro non troppo

BROTHER JAMES' AIR

BROTHER JAMES' AIR

Music by J.L. MACBETH BAIN
Words based on Psalm 23,
from the *Scottish Psalter*, 1650

CHRIST JESUS LAY IN DEATH'S STRONG BANDS
CHRIST LAG IN TODESBANDEN

Words by MARTIN LUTHER
Translated by RICHARD MASSIE
Music from *Geistliche Gesangbuchlein*
Harmonized by J.S. BACH

Solemnly

CHRIST THE LORD IS RISEN TODAY
EASTER HYMN

Words by CHARLES WESLEY
Music adapted from *Lyra Davidica*

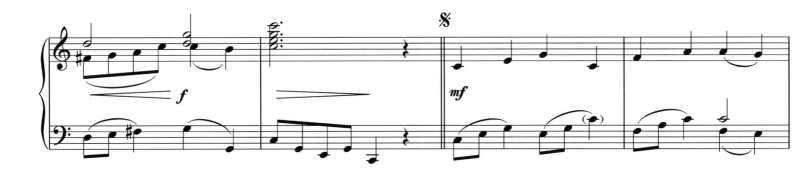

THE CHURCH'S ONE FOUNDATION

AURELIA

Words by SAMUEL JOHN STONE
Music by SAMUEL SEBASTIAN WESLEY

COME, YE FAITHFUL, RAISE THE STRAIN

ST. KEVIN

Words by JOHN OF DAMASCUS
Translated by JOHN MASON NEALE
Music by ARTHUR SEYMOUR SULLIVAN

CROWN HIM WITH MANY CROWNS

DIADEMATA

Words by MATTHEW BRIDGES
and GODFREY THRING
Music by GEORGE JOB ELVEY

THE DAY OF RESURRECTION

LANCASHIRE

Words by JOHN OF DAMASCUS
Translated by JOHN MASON NEALE
Music by HENRY THOMAS SMART

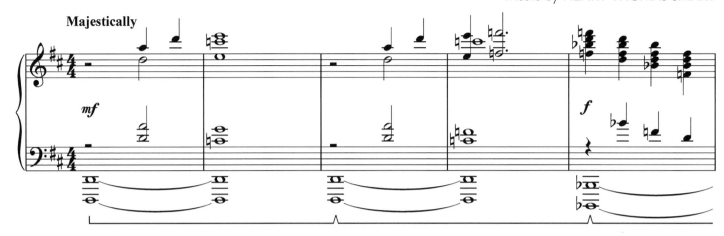

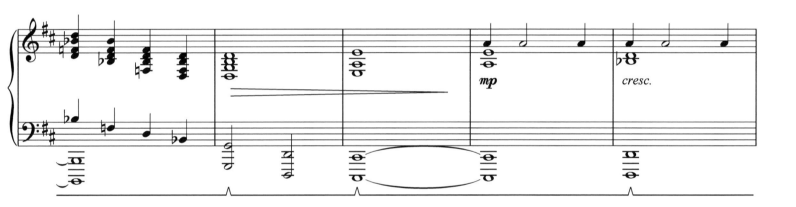

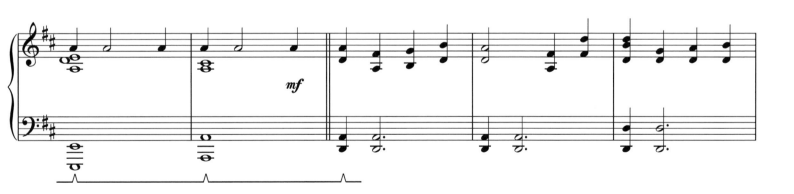

GLORIOUS THINGS OF THEE ARE SPOKEN

AUSTRIAN HYMN

Words by JOHN NEWTON
Music by FRANZ JOSEPH HAYDN

HALLELUJAH CHORUS
from MESSIAH

By GEORGE FRIDERIC HANDEL
1685–1759

Allegro moderato

I KNOW THAT MY REDEEMER LIVETH

from MESSIAH
excerpt

By GEORGE FRIDERIC HANDEL
1685–1759

THE HEAVENS DECLARE
(Psalm XIX)

By BENEDETTO MARCELLO
1686–1739

Maestoso, con moto

INTERMEZZO
from CAVALLERIA RUSTICANA

By PIETRO MASCAGNI
1863–1945

JESU, JOY OF MAN'S DESIRING
from CANTATA NO. 147

By JOHANN SEBASTIAN BACH
1685–1750

Moderato

IN THEE IS GLADNESS
IN DIR IST FREUDE

Words by JOHANN LINDEMANN
Translated by CATHERINE WINKWORTH
Music by GIOVANNI GIACOMO GASTOLDI

JESUS CHRIST IS RISEN TODAY
LLANFAIR

Words from *Lyrica Davidica*
Words for v. 4 by CHARLES WESLEY
Music by ROBERT WILLIAMS

JESUS SHALL REIGN
DUKE STREET

Words by ISAAC WATTS
Music by JOHN HATTON

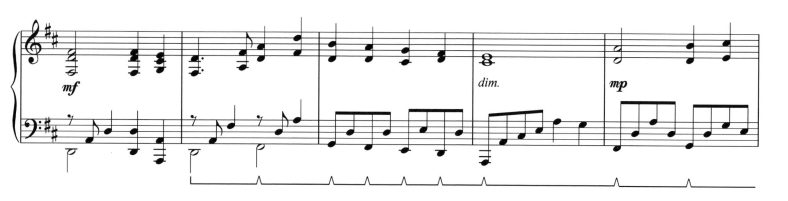

LA RÉJOUISSANCE
(The Rejoicing)
from MUSIC FOR THE ROYAL FIREWORKS

By GEORGE FRIDERIC HANDEL
1685–1759

LOOK, YE SAINTS, THE SIGHT IS GLORIOUS

BRYN CALFARIA

Words by THOMAS KELLY
Music by WILLIAM OWEN

NOW GOD BE PRAISED IN HEAVEN ABOVE

GELOBT SEI GOTT

By MELCHIOR VULPIUS

O SONS AND DAUGHTERS, LET US SING!

O FILII ET FILIAE

Words attributed to JEAN TISSERAND
Translated by JOHN M. NEALE
15th Century French Carol

O FOR A THOUSAND TONGUES TO SING

AZMON

Words by CHARLES WESLEY
Music by CARL G. GLÄSER

ODE TO JOY

from SYMPHONY NO. 9 IN D MINOR, Op. 125

By LUDWIG VAN BEETHOVEN
1770–1827

With spirit

RIGAUDON

By ANDRÉ CAMPRA
1660–1744

Maestoso, con moto

THINE IS THE GLORY

JUDAS MACCABEUS

Words by EDMOND LOUIS BUDRY
Music by GEORGE FRIDERIC HANDEL

With energy

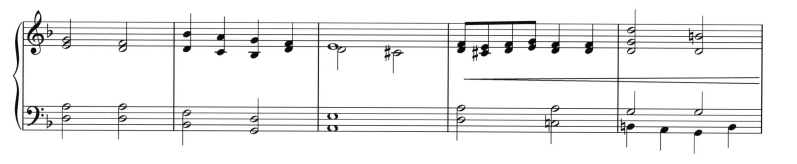

SHEEP MAY SAFELY GRAZE

from CANTATA NO. 208

By JOHANN SEBASTIAN BACH
1685–1750

THE STRIFE IS O'ER,
THE BATTLE DONE
VICTORY

Traditional Latin Text
Transcribed by FRANCIS POTT
Music by GIOVANNI P. DA PALESTRINA

THIS JOYFUL EASTERTIDE
VRUECHTEN

Words by GEORGE R. WOODWARD
Melody from *Psalmen*, 1685